Ten Poems
about Museums

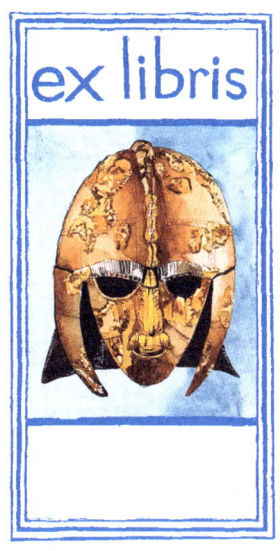

Candlestick Press

Published by:
Candlestick Press,
Diversity House, 72 Nottingham Road, Arnold, Nottingham NG5 6LF
www.candlestickpress.co.uk

Design and typesetting by Craig Twigg

Printed by Bayliss Printing Company Ltd of Worksop, UK

Selection and Introduction © David Clarke, 2024

Cover illustration © Jane Burn, 2024
https://janeburnpoet.wordpress.com/

Candlestick Press monogram © Barbara Shaw, 2008

© Candlestick Press, 2024

ISBN 978 1 913627 46 1

Acknowledgements

The poems in this pamphlet are reprinted from the following books, all by permission of the publishers listed unless stated otherwise. Every effort has been made to trace the copyright holders of the poems published in this book. The editor and publisher apologise if any material has been included without permission, or without the appropriate acknowledgement, and would be glad to be told of anyone who has not been consulted.

Thanks are due to all the copyright holders cited below for their kind permission.

Alice Brackenbury, *Then* (Carcanet Press, 2013). David Clarke, poem first appeared in this pamphlet. Glyn Edwards, *In Orbit* (Seren Books, 2023). Suzannah Evans, *Near Future* (Nine Arches Press, 2018). Helen Farish, *The Dog of Memory* (Bloodaxe Books, 2016) www.bloodaxebooks.com. Frances Horovitz, *Collected Poems: New Edition* (Bloodaxe Books, 2011) www.bloodaxebooks.com. Robert Minhinnick, *New Selected Poems* (Carcanet Press, 2012). Tom Sastry, *You have no normal country to return to* (Nine Arches Press, 2022). Lesley Saunders, *Divers: The Poetry Workshop Anthology* (Aark Arts, London and New Delhi, 2008) by kind permission of the author.

All permissions cleared courtesy of Dr Suzanne Fairless-Aitken – Swift Permissions swiftpermissions@gmail.com.

Where poets are no longer living, their dates are given.

Introduction

One of the things that makes us human is that we create or collect objects to surround ourselves with: our tools, our clothes, our art and our treasures. But what happens to all that stuff when we no longer need it? A lot of it will become rubbish, surplus to requirements. But if in the future people consider our possessions to be sufficiently important, beautiful or rare, they might end up being displayed in one of those special buildings we call a museum.

Museums are where we make sense of the past by looking at objects – but that can only happen when our imagination comes into play. When we stare into a glass case at an object made or found by another human being, who may have lived hundreds or perhaps even thousands of years ago, we are looking for traces of other lives. We wonder what realities people in the past inhabited and how they might connect with our own. Even when museums contain things humans haven't made, such as the bird in Thomas Hardy's poem 'In the Museum', it is our human relationship to time and history that we are trying to work out.

The poets whose work I have chosen sometimes question, as Helen Farish does, whether we can truly understand the lives of others through the objects that surrounded them. Or they wonder, like Tom Sastry, how future museum visitors will judge us from the things we leave behind. As this brief selection shows, museums are places for poets and their readers to time-travel in the imagination, where they can discover unexpected truths and possibilities.

David Clarke

In a Museum

Here's the mould of a musical bird long passed from light,
Which over the earth before man came was winging;
There's a contralto voice I heard last night,
That lodges in me still with its sweet singing.

Such a dream is Time that the coo of this ancient bird
Has perished not, but is blent, or will be blending
Mid visionless wilds of space with the voice that I heard,
In the full-fugued song of the universe unending.

Thomas Hardy (1840 – 1928)

The Fox in the National Museum of Wales

He scans the frames but doesn't stop,
the fox who has come to the museum today,
his eye in the Renaissance
and his brush in the Baroque.

Between dynasties his footprints
have still to fade, between the Shan and the Yung,
the porcelain atoms shivering at his touch,
ah, lighter than the emperor's breath, drinking rice wine from the bowl,
daintier than the eunuch pouring wine.

I came as quickly as I could
but already the fox had left the Industrial Revolution behind,
his eye has swept the age of atoms,
the Taj Mahal within the molecule.

The fox is in the fossils and the folios, I cry.
The fox is in Photography and the Folk Studies Department.
The fox is in the flux of the foyer,
the fox is in the flock,
the fox is in the flock.

Now the fox sniffs at the dodo
and at the door of Celtic orthography.
The grave-goods, the chariots, the gods of darkness,
he has made their acquaintance on previous occasions.

There, beneath the leatherbacked turtle he goes,
the turtle black as an oildrum,
under the skeleton of the whale he skedaddles,
the whalebone silver as bubblewrap.

Through the light of Provence moves the fox, through
the Ordovician era and the Sumerian summer,
greyblue the blush on him, this one who has seen so much,
blood on the bristles of his mouth,
and on his suit of iron filings the air fans like silk.

Through the Cubists and the Surrealists
this fox shimmies surreptitiously,
past the artist who has sawn himself in half
under the formaldehyde sky
goes this fox shiny as a silver
fax in his fox coat,
for at a foxtrot travels this fox
backwards and forwards in the museum.

Under the bells of *Brugmansia*
that lull the Ecuadoran botanists to sleep,
over the grey moss of Iceland
further and further goes this fox,
passing the lambs at the feet of Jesus,
through the tear in Dante's cloak.

How long have I legged it
after his legerdemain, this fox
in the labyrinth, this fox that never hurries
yet passes an age in a footfall, this fox
from the forest of the portrait gallery
to Engineering's cornfield sigh?

I will tell you this.
He is something to follow,
this red fellow.
This fox I foster –
he is the future.

No one else
has seen him yet.
But they are closing
the iron doors.

Robert Minhinnick

The Dark Museum

Here our most carefully curated darknesses
are sealed in their own tiny rooms. Feel free to disappear.
We remind you no smartphones, no flash photography.

We begin with dark bottled in the Arctic Circle
on a December afternoon, loud with creaking ice
flickering with soupy green aurora.

Neolithic dark, mined from the Black Forest
walls tattooed in geometric symbols
scratched by cave-dwellers with the horn of a wisent.

Hadopelagic dark from the Mariana Trench, almost silent –
a snowfall of remains from the bodies of dead whales
outlined in pulses of bioluminescence.

Cold-bone dark from Roman catacombs, left over
from last month's hallowe'en event. You may hear wailing
or the clanking of chains. This is not an interactive exhibit.

Newly acquired cultural darks: the resonant inner chambers
of a Stradivarius, the dusty mystery of J.D. Salinger's curtains.
The *noir* from film noir, soft as an old fedora.

Our Future Dark Simulation is sponsored by NASA.
After Earth's final power cut, a sunless solar system spins
purposeless rocks knocking in expanding space.

Suzannah Evans

DDR Museum

At best, they're not worth having. The Trabi
someone waited for, the Young Pioneer's scarf
the crackling fabric samples. We laugh
(glancing at the bug) call them *shabby*.

We're next in line to be revealed as fools
under the future's incredulous eyes.
They'll wonder how we bore it: lived the lies
read those papers, worked the petty rules.

What is our *Sandmännchen?* What will they keep
from England's shame, from being forever wrong –
our liberators with their kind ideas
and well-made things. They'll put the rest to sleep
in a museum. It won't belong
outside it. The life we know. Our fears.

Tom Sastry

Sun, Earth and Moon scale model

(Oxford Natural History Museum)

To stand together by the gallery
pillars looking down at Anning's
ichthyosaur, at a triceratops skull.
To imagine the air as a dense strata
filled with fossils. To notice then
two pinheads in a display case
and an explosion of scale beyond

comprehension. To hear you count
all nine zeros and read aloud that
there is a third sphere across the hall
the equivalent size and distance
of the sun. To see how you first flinch
then stare at the gilded ball and to know
what you will ask next. To tell you

there's one billion seconds in a decade
and to watch you translate our lives
into time, and to watch you transpose
time into distance, and to watch you lean
so close to the glass that your head
eclipses the painted earth, and its tiny,
textured moon, and to watch you.

Glyn Edwards

The Museum of Lincolnshire Life

Bobbins. Hooks and tools my father's
farming uncle might have had a use for.
Crazed china, stamped with coronation heads.

Green bottles dulled by patent medication.
Mangles. Smocks and dominoes. A copper
jelly mould shaped like a sleeping hare.

Fretwork. Caps. Bellows and trinkets in brass.
Abecedaries and bibles. Knives
and more knives, long unwhetted. Dust.

This is what gets left behind by creatures
who extend themselves in things – their bodies
worn against those handles and fraying seams,

stooped beneath the weight of all they made.
Yet here are piles of parlour music,
the yellow-toothed piano where they sang.

David Clarke

Museum Volunteer

Pulling on a pair of white duster gloves,
the kind mime artists wear for mustering
the long dead, she sits between cabinets

in this house of fragments, the small coin
of accidents poised in her palm, the act
of walking through walls about to begin,

then a worn silver face shines its moon
like a miniature torchbeam into the eyes
of a breathless crowd, the whole performance

perfect as birdsong heard under water or one
of those mornings when you can see thin air
tiptoeing towards you, a peep show of souls.

Lesley Saunders

The Wallace Collection

Not house, but jewel box. The first Duke
built it so he could blast at duck
in the dim marshes. Buses roar.
Who bought the art? Earls five and four.

The last, though loathed, crony to kings
outbid frantically at auction,
left landscape's blues, Our Lady's face,
forgotten in their packing case,
then died. His secretary, stunned,
found he was heir, the unclaimed son.

What filled the rooms? China's glazed glow,
bleu lapis, bleu céleste, bleu beau,
the last French queen's last desk, where clouds
of lilies swim the water's wood,
leafed with frail holly she could slam
when servants padded through her room.

Rococo gilt hides mercury.
Gilders, best paid, were first to die.
By Chelsea's lights the river smells.
Art draws, withdraws, bankrupts, compels.
The good son left to us the best
fine hands had formed, rough hands possessed,
bleu beau, bleu lapis, bleu céleste.

Alison Brackenbury

The '*bleus*' are the names of several generations of blue glaze for Sèvres porcelain.

Visit to the British Museum

You take me to the room of clocks
to see some long-dead master's
sleight of mind and hand.
Time thickens here, revolves,
regards itself in mirrors;
almost, each minute holds its place.
You tell me why one second hand
moves forward and not back,
explain escapement or the dead-beat pendulum.
All stars and days are measured here –
I think of loving and the seepage of our lives.

The Assyrians next;
a king hunts lions in bas-relief,
has hunted now for near three thousand years.
Would we be lovers beneath such brazen skies?
We swelter in the blood and din.
Time traps and baits us like these lions;
our moment is as transient as theirs.

Frances Horovitz (1938 – 1983)

In the Austrian Museum of Applied Arts

I picture a pear tree being felled,
a nearby boy with over-sized pockets
gathering its last fruit,
while the carpenter's tools
sharpen the light.

In the convent, the stool outlived
the remaining trees in the orchard
seven hundred years and counting.

But if a nun could come back
and join me by this exhibit,
'Goodness', she'd say, 'that old thing.
Where's the comb my father gave me,
the doll I kept all my life, the peace
I found, winter descending,
the snow closing in?'

Helen Farish